A Hell of Mercy

A Hell of Mercy

*A Meditation on Depression
and the Dark Night of the Soul*

TIM FARRINGTON

HarperOne
An Imprint of HarperCollins*Publishers*

HarperOne

This book first appeared in a shorter essay form, in *The Sun* magazine, in March 2001, through the kind and exceptionally patient attentions of Sy Safransky and Andrew Snee, who have all my gratitude.

I have used Mirabai Starr's wonderfully fresh rendering from the Spanish of San Juan's classic poem and his commentary on his verses in *The Dark Night*, except where otherwise noted. The faithful and excellent translation by Fathers Kieran Kavanaugh and Otilio Rodriguez, OCD, is still the indispensable scholarly version of the collected works of St. John of the Cross, and I have gratefully employed their state-of-the-art translations of *The Ascent of Mt. Carmel*, *The Spiritual Canticle*, and *The Living Flame of Love*.

HarperCollins books may be purchased for educational, business, or sales promotional use. For information please write: Special Markets Department, HarperCollins Publishers, 10 East 53rd Street, New York, NY 10022.

HarperCollins Web site: http://www.harpercollins.com

HarperCollins®, ▄®, and HarperOne™ are trademarks of HarperCollins Publishers.

FIRST EDITION

Interior design: Laura Lind Design

Library of Congress Cataloging-in-Publication Data is available upon request.
ISBN: 978–0–06–082518–8

08 09 10 11 12 QF 10 9 8 7 6 5 4 3 2 1

For my aunt, Sr. Mary Ann Farrington, SNJM, soul friend and true comrade on the path, and the only person I know whose copy of John's *Collected Works* is more beat-up than mine.

—WITH LOVE, AND GRATEFULLY

O dark dark dark. They all go into the dark ...
And we all go with them, into the silent funeral,
Nobody's funeral, for there is no one to bury.
I said to my soul, be still, and let the dark come upon you
Which shall be the darkness of God.

—T. S. ELIOT, "EAST COKER"

one

The house of my soul is too small for You;
may You enlarge it.
It is in ruins; may You restore it....
I am but dust and ashes:
yet suffer me to speak, through Your mercy.

—AUGUSTINE, *The Confessions,* CHAP. I

Depression began to weave itself into my life when I was seventeen: a classic "onset in late adolescence," I would learn years later, when I finally fell into professional hands. With neat soul logic, this was also the period in which I discovered Zen meditation. I spent my senior year of high school in Honolulu listening to the darker songs of the early Elton John, cutting calculus class to read D. T. Suzuki, slipping away to the Buddhist temple halfway up the Pali, and in general letting the warp and woof of my tidy American future unravel.

The depression was not incapacitating. It made it hard to take a lot of my suburban life seriously, but that was inextricably mingled with a growing consciousness of the larger brutalities of the world. Ethiopian children were starving on the evening news and genocide was mushrooming in Cambodia. Was I truly depressed or just awakening to the First Noble Truth of Buddhism, the insight that samsaric life is misery? My melancholy seemed like simple realism; if you weren't depressed, you obviously didn't know what was going on. I was becoming conscious of what Gurdjieff called "the horror of the situation." And so I took long walks and thought about death and the suffering of innocents. I wrote bad poetry. I did not go to Stanford.

—◆—

"A deeper enlightenment and wider experience than mine is necessary," the sixteenth-century Spanish Carmelite monk John of the Cross tells us in the prologue to his *Ascent of Mount Carmel,* "to explain the dark night through which a soul journeys toward God." He adds, "I am not undertaking this task because of any particular confidence in my own abilities. Rather, I am confident that the Lord will help me explain this matter, because it is necessary to so many souls."

It takes a certain kind of nerve to write a book like this. I am by no means an expert on either depression or what John called the dark night of the soul. I'm not a scholar, not a psychiatric professional, and certainly not a theologian. I'm more like a veteran, I suppose: a guy whose ass has been on the line, just one more guy with some stories from the front, someone who kept his head down as best he could and did what he had to when the shit hit the fan. It is certainly not my intention here to construct a simplistic one-to-one equation between what is called the dark night of the soul and what is called depression. That would be worse than foolish. *The Ascent of Mount Carmel* and its companion work, *The Dark Night of the Soul,* were originally written by John of the Cross for an audience that consisted solely of cloistered Carmelite nuns and monks. The books were the fruit of centuries of a rich and very specific

Christian contemplative tradition. Moreover, coming as they did at the watershed made by the Protestant Reformation and the violent reaction of the Catholic Church's Counter-Reformation—and the consequent, even for a time potentially fatal, suspicion of mystical and contemplative experience that permeated both camps and ultimately the secular paradigms as well—John's writings on the dark night would remain the state-of-the-art articulation of the condition through the succeeding centuries. They also remained until very recently the province of a select few, if not an elite.

In our own day the concept of the dark night of the soul has come into a much broader use. There is a marked tendency, in this period of (for better and for worse) mystical-contemplative revival and the popularization of spiritualities that were once the concern only of a highly dedicated minority, to make "the dark night" an easy label for anything ranging from a few bad days in a row to the death of a loved one. People now say they are going through a dark night in circumstances that used to be described merely as miserable, and we are beginning to hear the chorus of reaction as well, as various experts weigh in and bemoan the cheapening of the term.

Clearly, the danger of diluting a highly specific spiritual notion is real and present. Even in his own time John of the Cross himself was at great pains to distinguish the various nights of the soul from mere melancholia and what were then seen as bad humors. As "the dark night" gains increasing currency, the words, like any much-used coin, are rubbed smooth by rough usage and come to mean many things to many people. But this is true of any abstraction, from "the soul" to that ultimate Rorschach of a word, "God." It is true as well for "depression." The imprecision comes with the territory; and the vast country of human suffering remains what it has always been, the wilderness in which the soul must travel, whatever words we use for it. But I'm not writing this, in any case, for those looking to have their path precisely delineated; I'm writing for those whose maps have given out, as mine did along the way. God help me do it truly.

My spiritual naïveté at the age of eighteen was spectacular. I had the vaguest of adolescent notions that my elders had screwed up the world and that it was up to me to fix it. I had no humility whatsoever. I was a golden boy, a beloved oldest son, and I had never encountered any serious misery in my entire bright American life. My grandparents were all still alive and in good health. My father had survived Vietnam, and my parents' marriage had survived the sixties. Paula McCutchon breaking my heart in junior high was about as far as my experience of suffering reached.

My cluelessness, I see in retrospect, conferred a certain advantage on me. If we were smart, we might never become wise. Siddhartha Gautama, the son of the warrior King Suddhodana, was also raised in luxury and spared the soberings and distortions of early suffering. He was twenty-nine before his eyes were opened to the reality of human illness, aging, and death. (It took only a single ride down the road outside the palace; one wonders what roads he'd been traveling on before then.) A prince and a husband by then, he promptly abandoned kingdom and family to seek a solution. It was not the act of a prudent man. No doubt the Buddha at that point would have been diagnosed as something-or-other by a modern specialist; no doubt the man had issues. But off he went. Reality cannot wait for us to seek it without neurosis and an admixture of simple human foolishness. The tares of our flaws and delusions grow with the wheat of our honest need.

———

As I grew more serious about writing and spirituality through my young adulthood, I came to see depression as my shadow on the path; like the "black dog" of Churchill's recurrent blues, it was an inescapable presence. My lows could be debilitating, but they also seemed intimately related to my creativity itself and so were slightly glamorous, like Hemingway's alcoholism and Dostoyevsky's epilepsy. But my art at this time was self-indulgent stuff at best, graffiti on the cell wall of an unhappy self, and I invoked it much too readily to justify failures of character. I ruined a marriage, in no small part because my recurrent bouts of blackness were allied with a still untamed tendency to blame them on those closest to me. I graduated from bad poetry to bad short stories.

My spirituality, like that of many young Americans of my generation astonished and exhilarated to find themselves sailing the vast seas beyond their native Christianity, was of an exuberant and utterly undisciplined variety. The Beats' discovery of Zen was still rippling through the spiritual psyche of our country, and while a profound example of a deeply disciplined and committed Buddhist practice could be found in Gary Snyder, my own tastes ran more to Jack Kerouac's road-Zen and the wisdom of insecurity being stylishly practiced by Alan Watts on his Sausalito houseboat in spiritual concert with large amounts of excellent wine. I meditated when it pleased me and sought my ecstasies avidly; I was a transcendence junkie.

There's an old joke about a man walking in the mountains, enjoying the spectacular scenery, and as he's gaping at the great view he steps off a cliff. Luckily he manages to grab onto a tree root before he falls too far. As he's hanging there, too far down to climb back up, with a thousand-foot fall below him, he starts hollering, "Help! *Help!* Is anybody up there?" And a deep voice answers from above, "Yes, I'm up here."

And the guy calls, "Who's that?"

And the voice says, "It's me. God."

"Wonderful!" the guy says. "So, can you help me?"

And God says, "Sure, I can help you. You just have to have faith."

And of course the guy says, "Well, I do, I do, I have complete faith in you. But I'm starting to lose my grip here, so maybe you could just get on with the helping. Like, immediately."

"Okay," the Lord says. "Now, the first thing you do is let go and let God."

And the guy says, "I assume you mean that metaphorically."

"No, literally," God says. "It's an AA thing. Let go and let God. It's very simple. You just have to have faith."

So the guy looks down at the thousand-foot fall and thinks about it for a moment. Then he looks up again and says, "Well, is there anybody else up there?"

In the Gospels of my childhood Jesus had said over and over, "If anyone wishes to become a disciple of mine, let him take up his cross and follow me." But I didn't want a cross. I was looking for a second opinion.

———

I did not consider myself, on the whole, to be a depressed individual. "At first even admitting the fact of depression is difficult," Philip Martin writes in *The Zen Path Through Depression,* "because to do so seems tantamount to admitting that our view of ourselves is broken." To whatever degree I saw myself as broken, I believed I had embarked on the path to repair; I was frankly and unashamedly looking for the Meaning that would make me Whole. I had no teacher at this point, no discipline, no structure at all. I was a dharma bum, in my own mind, a free-form itinerant Beat-Zen monk, and life was my teacher. It would be quite some time before I was prepared to consider the devastating accuracy of Mariana Caplan's remark: "If life is the teacher, then there are a lot of bad students."

And so I muddled on: "I remained a haunted place, which gave me no rest, and from which I could not escape," as Augustine wrote of his own clueless youth in his *Confessions*. "For where could my heart flee from my heart? Where could I escape from myself? Where would I not dog my own footsteps? Still—I left my hometown."

two

To any person prepared to enter with respect
into the realm of his great and universal ignorance,
the secrets of being will eventually unfold,
and they will do so in a measure according to his freedom
from natural and indoctrinated shame
in his respect of their revelation.

—G. Spencer Brown, *The Laws of Form*

During the late seventies, having dropped out of Utah State University, I washed dishes at the campus cafeteria and pursued my own extreme and idiosyncratic studies in the library, reading everyone from Heraclitus to Kant and Freud and Derrida. I wrote feverish maverick papers, on Wittgenstein and Hamlet, getting out of what Wittgenstein called the fly bottle of language into true human action, and another on Wittgenstein and Nietzsche, the point of which I cannot for the life of me recall. But I'm sure it was very clever.

In this spirit I ransacked Western philosophy for years and came up more or less empty of the kind of realized wisdom I was looking for, though *The Myth of Sisyphus* may literally have saved my life. I spent the winter of 1978 on the coast of North Carolina in an unheated cottage, after a heartbreaking divorce and a halfhearted attempt to return to school at the University of Virginia, and Camus's first line, that the only real philosophical question is that of suicide, hit me right where I lived. I needed an act of God, some seed of unmistakable meaning I could cultivate, and I was within a minute or two of swimming out to sea if I didn't get it. I'd had it with the usual suspects; I wanted a genuine vocation or an early checkout, and a deserted beach community in the dead of winter was just the place to perform my all-or-nothing existential drama.

I was living on cornflakes and macaroni and cheese, and I was pretty whacked-out. I didn't talk to anyone for months and slept on my own eccentric schedule—approximately a twenty-five-hour day, cycling gradually through all manner of weird wake-up times. I had a half-serious theory that I was actually from another planet that had a longer day and that therefore my diurnal cycle was unfitted to Earth's twenty-four-hour rotation. It seemed as good a way as any to explain my complete out-of-syncness with everything mundane.

Eventually I did have a series of mystical experiences, as will happen if you make a sufficiently committed ascetic demand and put all your life chips on the table. The grain on the wood paneling came alive with universal meaning, and everything in my life made perfect sense for seven minutes; past and future were redeemed, and a warm glow suffused everything my blessed gaze rested on. And so forth. It is easy enough in retrospect to feel sheepish, and even cynical, about the experience given how recklessly I continued—and continue in many ways to this day—to squander the gift of conscious embodiment. But it did set a watermark of sorts: having passed once into the country of silence, I could in some sense never go back. I had only been a visitor to that silence, had not even begun to adjust my life toward actually trying to live there; but it gave me a glimmer of an inward direction and a taste of what I took to be God. It was enough at that point to keep me on the planet.

———

Unprepared to abide in stillness and sacred silence, and still whacked-out by social and sensory deprivation and the asceticism of macaroni and cheese, I also went through a phase of hearing voices, including one that identified itself as Jesus as an old man. I'd been reading Ferlinghetti's marvelous poem "Christ Climbed Down" and was primed for the notion of a renunciation of the crucifixion—wishful thinking, I see now, but certainly worth a try. A cross is a bad career move, spiritually speaking. It's agony, not edification—involuntary, humiliating, and ultimately ruinous—and anyone with any sense or choice in the matter will dodge it if they can. Even Jesus prayed, the night before his death, "Father, if it be your will, take this cup away from me."

The Jesus-climbed-down voice fortunately lent itself to transcription, and I ended up writing an incredibly pretentious novel, a sort of first-person anti-Gospel: "My name is Jesus. I am an old man now," it began. Yikes.

The book was bad, but it was good in the sense of being better than suicide, and after a while the voices faded to a dim roar and I began to write merely puerile bad novels in a more standard fashion and eventually went back to Utah and married my first wife again and we lived relatively un-eventfully, and even happily, she getting graduate degrees in mathematics and I writing very bad novels that no one at all ever read, for some four years after that. And every once in a while at my writing desk that sacred silence would come upon me anew and all my fruitless frantic efforts would seem redeemed in simple being. That holy hush seemed to have little effect in my actual life, but like some divine version of variable-rate reinforcement it did keep me coming back to my writing desk day after day. Get thee to thy cell, and thy cell will teach thee everything, as the old desert fathers told the new monks; or, as Camus put it, one must imagine Sisyphus happy. Sustained by intermittent tastes of silence, I developed an extraordinary tolerance for futility—

content more or less to push my writing rock a bit more up the endless hill every morning. At least it kept me off the streets, no small contribution to society in its own right.

It was during this domestic phase that I first considered the possibility that I needed biochemical help. I remained inexplicable to myself, and my sense of having failed to find an illuminating context was sharper than ever. By then I was ransacking Western psychology as avidly as I had ransacked philosophy. B. F. Skinner was all the rage at that time, but I was not prepared to consider that my angst could be soothed into pigeonlike contentment through behavioral modification. I had dutifully strained my dreams through a Freudian sieve and found no help in the vicissitudes of my fairly standard id. The various cognitive theories emerging then struck me as too peppy and overly oriented toward social adjustment. Abraham Maslow's enthusiastic psychology of self-actualization held a certain appeal but seemed to leave out what was most obvious to me, which was an abiding existential misery. My soul was starved for Something, I had no idea what, and the pain of that hunger had made me desperate enough to consider even a hypothesis as fundamentally loathsome to me as the possibility that the Something was merely chemical in nature.

Of course, as Andrew Solomon points out in his marvelous book on depression, *The Noonday Demon,* "Everything about a person is chemical if one wants to think in those terms. The sun shines brightly and that's just chemical too, and it's chemical that rocks are hard, and that the sea is salt, and that certain springtime afternoons carry in their gentle breezes a quality of nostalgia that stirs the heart to longings...." He quotes a fellow sufferer of manic depression, Maggie Robbins: "You can say it's 'just chemistry.' I say there's nothing 'just' about chemistry."

Jesus had a biochemistry. The Word was made flesh. We have not even begun to properly understand what it means that biocarbons have arranged themselves on this planet in such a way as to know that they are fleeting, finite assemblages born to suffer, love, and die. "Just chemical" is a way to baffle the terror of that mystery with the music of a seeming certainty; it is a campfire story posing as an explanation, the centerpiece of what David McDowell of Columbia University calls "modern neuromythology."

I mean, really: "Just chemical." Say the words out loud as often as you please; say them while driving to malls and funerals, in fast-food lines and at wedding feasts, in rain, despair, gratuitous joy, and earthquake; say them when your children are born and when your parents die; say them while turning rosary beads and during the fifth game of the NBA finals and at that moment two hours before dawn when there's nothing but you and the ticking clock: "Just chemical." You'll still have to get out of bed tomorrow as a mammal starved for meaning.

Still, one cannot stray far from what passes for normal consciousness in our culture without encountering the guardian deities of medication. At that point in the late seventies, lithium was the state-of-the-art antidepressant, and the perverse simplicity of the notion that a minuscule failure of electrolytic salt lay at the root of my intricate suffering was almost dizzying. I tried it briefly and found what every artist fears from psychiatry to be true: the drug interfered with my writing. I felt blunted and dim on lithium, displaced about three feet from the center of myself, a gray bystander to my essential life. And so I stopped taking the stuff—"Dog don't eat what dog don't like," as a writer friend put it succinctly—and took my unmedicated chances.

It was at about this time that I read Kay Redfield Jamison's *Touched with Fire,* a fascinating study of "manic-depression and the artistic temperament." In appendix B, Jamison assembled an imposing list of "Writers, Artists, and Composers with Probable Cyclothymia, Major Depression, or Manic-depressive Illness." Many of the names on the list had a ·, a ∅, a †, or some combination of the three beside them. The · symbolized time in an asylum or psychiatric hospital, ∅ denoted a suicide attempt, and a † meant the artist had killed him- or herself. Thus T. S. Eliot and William Faulkner had gotten off relatively easy with mere ·s; Hermann Hesse had both a · and a ∅, and Sylvia Plath, among others, had hit the trifecta: ·, ∅, †.

It was heady company. I already had a · of my own; I had toyed seriously enough with my ∅; and for all I knew it was just a matter of time before I registered my †. But I didn't see any way out of it. It seemed like the price of art.

three

Ego thinks it is much more powerful than it actually is. In this way it defends itself against the realization of its true condition ... which is fucked.

—ROBERT HALL

Depression saps relationships; untreated depression eventually destroys them. It may be harder to live with a person who is irredeemably miserable than it is to be the locus of such misery yourself. The cumulative effect of my condition took its intimate toll in the long run, and my first marriage fell apart for the second time. By then my theories on my existential condition had taken a turn for the cosmic and I made my way to California, seeking the solace of fellow pilgrims and eccentrics, and duly discovered the burgeoning New Age.

Amid such metaphysical largesse, my views on depression gradually acquired the intricacy of the jury-rigged. I considered counterproductive patterns laid down during reckless past lives, got political for a while and was arrested outside the nuclear laboratories in Livermore, and attended a dream institute on Shattuck Avenue where the interpretive methods were based on a combination of Jungian philosophy and the dreaming ways of the Senoi tribe of Malaysia. I studied Esperanto briefly for some reason but stopped when I realized that the only other people speaking it were sweet, well-heeled sixty-five-year-old women given to drinking lots of tea. If the women had been younger or even drunk beer, I suppose I might be speaking Esperanto still, but my idealism went only so far.

I was living then with a guy named Richard, a besotted composer of modernistic music, and his cat, Angela. In the mornings I would work on my bad novel in progress and Richard would sit at the rented piano in the living room to "compose." He was blocked, he said, and he would work up to the creative leap through a set of bizarre breathing exercises that culminated in an unnerving series of hoots, *hunh*s, and visceral groans, at which point he would abruptly begin to pound the piano like a three-year-old pretending to be Beethoven, except that his dissonance was more disciplined. He had known John Cage in New York and had run with the fast crowd in his youth, but something had gone wrong. At fifty-eight he had lost all his teeth, and I never saw him eat. He lived on cigarettes and some kind of amphetamines, with a vodka nightcap. How he had survived so long, I have no idea. But every once in a while he would suddenly play Bach, apparently just for the hell of it, exquisitely, and the shabby house would be filled for a while with magic.

At those moments I felt all the beauty and nobility of a life consecrated heedlessly to art. But those breathing exercises scared me, as did his horrific dentures. Terrified that I was looking at a grotesquely foreshortened image of myself some thirty years down the road, I began brushing my teeth religiously five times a day, and when I bogged down in my own sad efforts to make art and found myself actually considering doing some of Richard's breathing exercises to break the blockage, I panicked.

It is something that happens to many aspiring young writers, I suspect: that moment of truth when the abysmal path ahead shows itself in all its yawning and dangerous profundity and you realize that you're almost certainly not up to it, not up to the poverty and the obscurity, the uncertainties and indignities, the haunting of failure and the lack of a dental plan. Some people go back to school at that point, get their MFA, and eventually teach; some go into business and promise themselves they will write someday when they are financially secure. But I felt that my own bridges back to such reassuring normality had burned long since, and, being the melodramatic mystical sort that I am, I went into a monastery instead.

The dark night of the soul, John of the Cross emphasizes, is not something that happens to spiritual beginners. Most beginners—which I certainly was when I began my two years at the Siddha Yoga ashram at the corner of Stanford and San Pablo Avenues in Oakland, despite almost a decade of half-assed Zen practice—are in the happy condition of having just discovered something, of having glimpsed the Light, and of being drawn onto the path toward its realization: They "feel such passion about divine things and are so devoted to their spiritual practices!" as John notes indulgently. "They bask in their bounty." The early stages of the spiritual life are filled with vigorous resolutions and earnest, hopeful work on oneself; a sense of possibility prevails, and the infusion of buoyant energy leads to a heady expansion, to a joyous sense of moving steadily toward the radiant goal. We see a transformed self emerging, a better self, progressing more or less systematically toward perfection. Within the natural cycles of ups and downs, of relative dry spells and plateaus succeeded by periods of breakthrough and renewed illumination, this honeymoon phase of the spiritual life can last for years. In certain personality types it can even last a lifetime.

For others, though, this initial surge toward the Light passes sooner or later into an unnerving ebb. The sustaining spiritual energy is inexplicably withdrawn; the tide of illumination recedes. The self that floated so happily on the divine profusion runs aground on the freshly exposed rocks of unregenerate personality. There is a shocking sense of regression, of seemingly transcended character flaws reasserting themselves more strongly than ever. Having striven to eliminate our pathological self-condemnation in the interests of building a healthy self-acceptance, we may find that our self-condemnation has been the main thing keeping our megalomania in check. Our worldly ambition, renounced for the sake of humility and spiritual simplicity, turns out to be the thing that paid the rent and sent the kids to college. The mediocrity of our marriage, savagely and courageously exposed in the heady expansion of the self's craving for authenticity, is revealed to have been the mask for our fundamental failure to be interesting, and now we have alimony to pay to boot.

And so on. We are jury-rigged creatures, psychically; one cannot start down the road of undoing the self's slapdash constructions without the whole structure starting to creak and yield. There seems to be no end to the unpleasant internal quick fixes that are exposed as we tear away the drywall of our former normality, and the spiritual self, confronted with the mortifying ongoing substratum of the old, unspiritual self, finds the contrast far more painful in the light of the ideal vision glimpsed and cherished and more or less identified with during the honeymoon phase of the remodeling.

In the ashram I hit this wall of ego reality abruptly, like a bird flying into a plate-glass window, after about six months of zealous chanting, meditation, and the chopping of endless vegetables. Paradoxically enough, it was in the library of this missionary outpost of Western Hinduism, ostensibly immersed in the exuberant Advaita philosophy of Kashmir Shaivism, that after some desperate rummaging through the Bhagavad Gita, the *Shiva Sutras,* Patanjali, and Ramana Maharshi, I discovered the neglected depth of Christian mysticism in *The Cloud of Unknowing* and first considered my inner distress in the light of what John of the Cross called the dark night of the soul. St. John's doctrine of how one may "unburden [oneself] of all earthly things, avoid spiritual obstacles, and live in that complete nakedness and freedom of spirit necessary for divine union" is notoriously difficult, but he summarizes its essence graph-ically in the "Sketch of Mount Carmel," a drawing he first made for the Carmelite nuns in Beas, whose confessor he was from 1579 to 1581. In this schematic, the central path of "the perfect spirit" to the summit of Monte Carmelo, symbolizing union with God, is labeled simply as "*nada nada nada nada nada nada y au en el Monte nada*": noth-ing, more nothing, and even on the Mount, nothing.

I was more or less prepared to see that nothing as a good thing. I associated it with the numinous hush, the sweet silence that often came upon me at my writing desk and in meditation: Our nada who art in nada, nada be thy name. In any case, I had little choice but to embrace the holy nothing at that point: all my somethings, even my spiritual somethings, had crapped out.

In ashram culture, a good working misery was often called "burning," as in burning off the soul's impediments and debris, and a depression that didn't keep you from chopping vegetables and chanting was thought to be an excellent thing for one's karma. It is not actually such a stretch to consider depression as an involuntary form of postmodern mortification, a salutary humiliation akin to a hair shirt. We abhor the pathological penances practiced by what we smugly think of as medieval fanatics, but what if there was a baby in those fanatics' bathwater? It is easy enough to see the morbid ambition in brutal self-denial and flagellation, but many genuine truths turn grotesque, blown up to hyperpopular size. (Think of judging contemporary music by the halftime show at the Super Bowl.) What if some degree of pained and penitential consciousness, of realized inadequacy in the light of the sacred, is in fact necessary to the full human life? Our depressions, which we labor so to cure before they disrupt our self-enclosed routines, may be nefarious blessings, gestures by our stymied souls toward the conscious embrace of helplessness and suffering.

And so, in the champa-scented silence of the meditation hall at 4 a.m., surrounded by images of Shiva, Ganesh, and Saraswati, with the occasional gunshot highlighting the Oakland streets outside, I began to ease through my dryness, emptiness, and panic into a relationship with what Meister Eckhart called "the God beyond 'God,'" with the palpable Mystery pulsing where the words gave out. And every once in a while the country of silence would open to me like a flower to a bee and my buzzing mind would cease to pain me.

Meanwhile, I was a good ashram citizen. I chopped and chanted and did my mantra *japa* on my little wristlet of *rudraksha* beads, and in the afternoons I slipped away to the library and read *The Cloud of Unknowing* and *The Dark Night of the Soul.* The Siddha Yoga ashram's particular tradition had a livid streak of kundalini emphasis running through it like a lava flow, and during the weekend "intensives," the guru would circulate the hall transmitting the dynamic spiritual energy through what was called *shaktipat.* It was considered auspicious to go into a Hindu version of St. Vitus' Dance as a result of *shaktipat,* and many of my fellow seekers would duly succumb to all manner of spiritually energized behavior, spasms, oinks, and bleats, soul-induced gyrations, and auspicious bops.

It was sort of Pentecostal. But by the end of my first year in the ashram I'd had it with my damn kundalini. All I wanted was for my soul to simplify itself and for my mind to shut up. I would dive for the silence and just sit there, like a happy rock, the deaf, dumb, and blind guy in the country of the ecstatic. Once some guy across the room started hollering, "I'm God! *I'm God!*" and I just thought, Yeah, yeah, keep it to yourself. The ushers led him away and gave him a banana to try to ground him, but you could still hear him hollering from the lobby, "I'm God! I don't *want* a banana! I'm *God!*" I suppose I felt superior, ensconced in what I took to be the throes of my dark night, but God has a way of humbling us all in the long run. Years later, during a mania, also suspecting that I was God, I climbed naked onto a huge cross on a hill above some mission church in Arizona, to the dismay of the pilgrims below, as part of a very precise postapocalyptic mission sixty thousand years in the future. At that point, I needed a whole bunch of bananas myself.

"When we seek enlightenment to avoid our suffering, we are fleeing from the stark terror of accepting reality as it is—the stark terror that is beyond our ability to grasp but is always there," Mariana Caplan writes, dissecting the varieties of spiritual pretension in her wonderfully lucid book, *Halfway Up the Mountain*. "If we know we are seeking enlightenment because reality is so hard to bear, we at least have an intuitive sense of what we are fleeing from: a reality that has already begun to surface in our consciousness—a reality that our very seeking will eventually cause us to face."

A monastery joke: There's this guy who is completely burned out, fed up with the world, and he decides to spend the rest of his life as a hermit in a contemplative monastery. His abbot warns him he will have to take a vow of silence, that he will be allowed to say only two words every ten years. And the man replies, "No problem." The abbot says, "Okay, that's it for the next ten years then."

So the guy shaves his head and puts on his robes and retires to his cell, and for ten years he keeps perfect silence.

After the first decade the abbot calls him in for his two words, and the man comes in with his ribs poking out and his cheeks sunken and says, "Food cold." And the abbot gives him his blessing and a warm meal and sends him back to his cell.

Another ten years go by, not a word out of the guy. And then he is once again ushered into the abbot's office for his once-a-decade speech, and this time he drags himself in with big black bags under his bloodshot eyes and says, "Bed hard." And the abbot gives him his blessing and a camping pad for the bed and sends him back to his cell.

Another ten years of utter silence go by, and once again the abbot sends for the man. And this time the guy staggers in covered with boils and flea bites and says, "I quit!" And the abbot says, "I'm not surprised. Frankly, you've done nothing but bitch and moan since you got here."

I had entered the ashram demoralized by failed relationships, panicked by the realities of committing my life to art, and appalled by the chaos and poverty of my inner and outer lives. And also, of course, looking for God. It would be easy enough to shoot the fish in the barrel of my childish notions of transcendence and my wish fantasies of solving life's misery by cutting a quick and dirty deal with the divine. I suppose it was worth a try; and you're only young once. But frankly, the food was cold and the bed was hard.

In any case, mercifully enough, the finality of a monastic renunciation of both art and intimacy proved beyond my reach. After about a year and a half in the ashram, I found myself scribbling poetry on the backs of envelopes in the bathroom and slipping off to the McDonald's down San Pablo Avenue to eat cheeseburgers and read Doris Lessing novels, and in time I ran off with the monastery's cook, a tough old veteran of the Indian ashram with a magnificently low tolerance for bullshit. We spent three seasons in a tiny shack in the mountains of Mendocino County chanting, meditating, and clearing poison oak and barbed blackberry brush from old paths in the third-growth forest, and the mortifications of institutional monastic life pale in comparison. She eventually went back to India—to work with Mother Teresa, I believe—and I worked for a while in a lumber mill in Willits before returning to the Bay Area, chastened by hardship, if not particularly wiser, and grateful for hot running water and corner stores.

John of the Cross's *Dark Night of the Soul* and the third edition of the American Psychiatric Association's *Diagnostic and Statistical Manual of Mental Disorders* were my faithful companions by now: I still had no idea whether I was making my blind way to God through the cloud of unknowing or was just clinically fucked-up. In any case, I made the most of what California had, peculiarly, to offer. I lived alone in stark rented rooms, writing stark little tales of spiritual failure, and I lived in a commune in the Haight, where I wrote bright false utopian nonsense. I did dreamwork and yoga, read Ken Wilber and the Bhagavad Gita, meditated and integrated and ate according to sophisticated plans, and through it all I was intermittently depressed in a way that no technique or philosophy could touch. In the spirit of the times, I self-medicated with marijuana and the occasional hallucinogen, which given my biochemistry added a religiously tinged lunacy to the already volatile stew. I had experienced enough of the inherent nonsectarian pathology of all well-meaning human institutions in the ashram to begin the long process of forgiveness toward my own Mother Church, and I found my way back to a Catholicism of sorts in the early nineties, discovered the contemporary Centering Prayer movement, and traded in my Sanskrit mantra for a Sacred Word without much affecting the deep ongoing obscurity of my meditation.

I was hospitalized twice, once for depression and once for mania, and so in addition to the half-lotus and *pranayama,* I became acquainted with Haldol and four-point restraints. And still I persisted in the belief that my condition was manageable, that I was more or less steering the careening vehicle of my life. That is, until my mother died, terribly, of stomach cancer, in the winter of my forty-first year. That was when the wheels came off.

four

Woe unto you that desire the day of the Lord!
To what end is it for you? The day of the Lord
is darkness, and not light,
As if a man did flee from a lion, and a bear met him.

—AMOS 5:18–19

There are things you simply cannot prepare for. This is not something anyone really wants to hear. We spend our lives preparing; we stake our pride on mastering the troublesome aspects of our world. We study, we practice, we polish and adjust; even our earnest efforts to "go with the flow" and humbly surrender to the processes of a life force larger than ourselves are invariably suffused with a hidden agenda. If we are good, bad things will not happen; if we are good enough, our suffering will end. All our labors, spiritual and secular alike, are directed toward achieving a condition of cosmic competence, and practice makes perfect.

But the dark night, as John of the Cross knew well, is not about how good we are, or even how good we can get. The dark night takes our goodness like a handful of dry leaves and crumbles it into dust. It shows us that we can never be good enough. "If I should wash myself with snow and cleanse my hands with lye," cries Job, the most righteous man on earth, to the Lord in the first bitterness of his incomprehensible affliction, "yet you would plunge me in the ditch, so that my own clothes would abhor me." It is not the cry of a man enjoying a "growth experience."

You don't need to retire to a cloister or the desert for years on end to experience a true dark night; you don't even have to be pursuing any particular "spiritual" path. Raising a challenged child, or caring for a failing parent for years on end, is at least as purgative as donning robes and shaving one's head; to endure a mediocre work situation for the sake of the paycheck that sustains a family demands at least as much in the way of daily surrender as years of pristine silence in a monastery. No one can know in advance how and where the night will come, and what form God's darkness will take. The soul is purged of its presumptions and illusions in the fire that it finds, wherever and whatever that fire may be. And no soul, once it feels the heat of that fire, wants to be there. The essence of the dark night is the arrival at the heart of human helplessness, the conscious realization of being immersed in a fire of misery so hot it burns away our every attempt at a remedy or escape.

In our day of endless how-tos for the seeker of sacred competence, I don't think the involuntary nature of this plunge into the spiritual flame is sufficiently emphasized. The dark night is not something we do on purpose. Our purposes, indeed, are one of the main blocks to the work the dark night has to accomplish. "The goal that promises to bring 'healing' and completion, is beyond all measure strange to consciousness," Jung says, "and can find entrance into consciousness only with the greatest difficulty. This cannot happen except under compulsion, and the compulsion always attaches itself to a life situation in which the individual does not know how to help himself in any other way."

The "way" we do not know is darkness to our mind. It is not what we signed up for, setting out on the shining path with such high hopes. Everyone wants to see the Light. But Moses hid his head in a cleft of rock when God passed near, simply to survive the encounter. Saul of Tarsus, on his way to Damascus, was literally blinded by the glare of God and had to be led by hand into the city, where he spent the next three days in anguished eclipse, unable even to eat or drink. "It is a terrible thing," he later wrote, as Paul, in his letter to the Hebrews, "to fall into the hands of the living God."

◆

Whatever there is of love and tenderness and wisdom in my life owes something to my mother. She was an astonishing person with a tremendous heart and a real gift for empathy and rapport, a gifted actress who taught drama, and a nonstop storyteller with an unrelenting eye for the telling detail. I was nuts at her funeral, but one of the best things I did was stay after the cemetery ritual was over and everyone else had gone off to eat casseroles. It was pouring rain, a forty-degree January day, and I had taken off my coat and tie and was hanging with the grave diggers, a wonderful old black man on a backhoe, and his son-in-law. They let me help them take down the awning and roll up the fake green grass surface and fold the chairs; I actually cranked the casket into the ground myself and wielded a shovel to fill the hole. It was the sanest I'd been for days, and the sanest I would be for weeks.

When we had the grave filled, we stomped around the edges to tamp the dirt down, a wild slow dance. I have no idea what those two guys made of this poor undone white guy, but I have never been treated with more gentle kindness, respect, and compassion.

The funny thing is, I actually did catch pneumonia that day, the "death of cold" that all mothers warn their children against; and a few weeks later while in the grip of the pneumonia I wrapped my car around a concrete irrigation piling in a fruit orchard off Highway 99 south of Chico in the Sacramento Valley and almost died. I remember losing it on the wet road and sliding sideways into the orchard: the timeless moment of it, the calm and lucidity and peace of being quite sure I'd accomplished my barely subliminal (I started smoking the day my mother died) suicide mission. I hit the piling sideways, on the driver's side, and crumpled the car into a **C** shape that left no apparent place for a human body; it knocked me out cold, and when I woke up a bunch of men were standing around the vehicle discussing whether I was dead and whether the car was going to blow up. The engine, miraculously, was still running; all the damage was centered just behind the driver's-side door, and that foot-and-a-half variation from dead center saved my life. The backseat ended up in the trunk. My back hurt terribly, and I was pretty sure I'd ruptured my spleen. (I hadn't, as it turned out, and they tell me you can do without your spleen anyway.) The ambulance arrived, and everyone marveled at how lucky I was to be alive and so forth. The police report concluded mildly enough that I had been driving faster than weather conditions warranted, which I thought was a very gentle way of pointing out what a death-courting maniac I was at that point.

⌣

Eventually, mercifully, the mania of grief subsided. The depression in which I found myself mired after the death of my mother was different from my earlier depressive episodes: different in intensity and, most crucially, in duration. My life had always been peppered with black days, days in which taking a shower seemed far beyond my means, days in which I just hunkered down like a wounded beast and endured; I'd had black weeks and even the occasional black month. During a particularly trying time in the early nineties, I'd spent an entire summer staring at the blinking cursor on my computer screen, as if at a receding satellite; unable to write a word, I'd been reduced to reading Job, the Psalms of anguish, and Jeremiah's Lamentations ("He has beset me round about with bitterness and grief, and left me to dwell in the dark like those long dead...."). Bernadette Roberts's classic book *The Path to No-Self*, a blessedly lucid account of the dark night's debilitations and ultimate fruition, was a great help to me. I steered by passages such as, "Eventually, I learned that the best protection against this pain was to fully accept it, and that by virtually sinking into it, sinking into my feeling of utter misery and nothingness, the pain lost much of its punch." With the writings of St. John of the Cross, hers was the only survival manual I had found.

But now the manuals were no help; my spiritual library, crammed with the wisdom of the ages, was useless to me. I might as well have been collecting detective novels all those years. Indeed, as the blackness deepened and went on, detective novels were all that I could read. The fact that I found Sue Grafton more appealing than the saints and mystics only deepened my sense that I had lost it completely.

At this point in the process, it was easy enough to suspect that what I was going through was "just grief." It is true that it is often the loss of a loved one that precipitates the most severe purgations of the dark night. But as there is no such thing as "just biochemistry," there is no such thing as just grief. Grief and the experience of loss in depth get so little space in our world; out of fear of morbidity, or debilitation, we are often encouraged to buck up, to get over it, and so to throw out the baby of the slow true process of grieving with the bathwater. Grief will never go away, if we're really paying attention. It's part of being awake: we love, and we lose those we love to the erosions of time, sickness, and death (until those we love lose us to the same). To lose a loved one is to be called to come to genuine terms with that loss, or risk losing touch with that in us which loved.

Whether you are truly in a "dark night" or "just" grieving is a question that I have come to believe is insoluble in the midst of the process. The two experiences can certainly intertwine; often the loss of a loved one exposes the superficiality of the spiritual notions we believed to be sustaining us and challenges us to let go of them and go deeper; and the dark night, teaching us to let go of protective ideologies, often allows us to open for the first time to the nakedness of our real suffering of the death of loved ones. God uses our helplessness where it arises, and few things bring our human helplessness home to us more sharply and unavoidably than grief. To the extent that we have been deferring our sense of mortal vulnerability, the experience of true grief, of our honest and natural emotional response to real loss, can come as a revelation and can set us free. But first we must learn to ignore the chorus of prudent voices urging us to get our grieving done on the world's timetable and move on with our bright effective lives. Grief's work is slow work; it is done in God's quiet time; and it requires nothing more of us than our consecrated and surrendered attention. It's not trying to accomplish anything, really; it just wants us to know that grief is love too.

In any case, by this time my depression had passed beyond its initial occasion in the fact that my mother had spent the last night of her life vomiting an evil-smelling brew of diarrhea-like bile every five minutes; that she had finally, inevitably, choked on the stuff; that she had died in my arms with her clear blue eyes gazing at me in an absolutely mystifying peace, with nothing between us except death. It had passed beyond the fact that my puny career was in the crapper, that my books had sunk from sight without a ripple. It had passed even beyond the knowledge that I too was going to die someday and that everyone I knew and loved was going to die. My depression by now was general and undiscriminating.

"It is one of the paradoxes of transformation that the closer we get to new possibility, the worse things tend to seem," Richard Moss writes in *The Black Butterfly*. In another of the paradoxes of transformation, however, I found no comfort at all in this notion. I was haunting the bookstores, looking desperately for some help, but the spiritual books all seemed like chatter now. The universe had simplified itself into a desert of meaningless suffering, and the wisest words were just marks on the bleached expanse. Joy, compassion, peace, and the divine: yadda-yadda-yadda. Even the authors trying to buck me up with insights into the difficulties of the path had obviously never really been through a blackness quite like this. It was the same old shit, and none of it helped. Darkness was my only friend. But I didn't like darkness. I wished he'd go away.

For what it was worth, John of the Cross had warned me of this long in advance: "The soul finds no solace or support in any doctrine or spiritual teacher. This dark night brings solitude and desolation with it.... Rather than being consoled [by the efforts of spiritual guides], the soul's suffering is intensified. She knows there is no hope, no cure, no release from affliction" (*The Dark Night,* II, 7:3). With characteristic frankness, John adds, "And in truth, there is no way out. Until God finishes purifying the soul in the way he desires to do it, no remedy can heal her nor is there relief from her pain."

The reality at this point in the process is no comfort: "She is as powerless as someone imprisoned in a dark dungeon, bound hand and foot, unable to move, who cannot see or feel any favor from above or below. She remains like this until her spirit is humbled, softened, and purified, until she becomes so subtle, so simple, and so refined that she can become one with the Spirit of God." And again, with seeming ruthlessness, John blithely adds, "If it is authentic, the process will last for a number of years."

five

It's terrible to think that all I've suffered,
and all the suffering I've caused,
might have arisen from the lack of a little salt in my brain.
—ROBERT LOWELL, OF HIS MANIC DEPRESSION

"At the first-order level of experiential description,"
Denys Turner notes in *The Darkness of God*, "John
of the Cross's accounts of the sufferings of the 'dark nights
of the soul' are uncannily similar to what a person will
give from the inside of depression." The truth of this is in-
disputable. The American Psychological Association lists
nine diagnostic criteria for a major depressive episode, at
least five of which must be present during the same two-
week period, representing "a change from previous func-
tioning." These range from "depressed mood, most of the
day, nearly every day" through anhedonia to fatigue, feel-
ings of worthlessness, and suicidal ideation. Even a cursory

glance through John's vivid symptomatology of dryness, devastation, and despair will confirm that we are in the same country here.

The congruity may seem potentially devastating in our reductionistic age. It is terrible enough to fall into the hands of a living God without the torment of trying to decide whether one is in a "true" dark night or whether it is "just depression." To a vulnerable self suffering a crisis of such depth, the thought that all the agony is just the wasted motion of biochemical atoms may itself be enough to bring on thoughts of suicide. It is pointlessness that we fear most.

Yet there is no way around the mortifying consideration. Humility dictates that we not ignore psychological and biological factors, and simple realism may require that we seek professional help. That said, it must also be noted that there is as much danger in relying too much on socially sanctioned psychiatry as there is in erring on side of the biochemically naked soul risking the world undrugged. Having stumbled through the halls of the medical psychiatric system myself, I've seen too clearly how easy it is to let "patient" and "pill taker" become the consuming whole of one's working identity. Nothing will screw you up more than a team of professionals determined to help you.

Except, perhaps, believing that therapy and medicine can offer us no help at all. The fact that you're depressed doesn't necessarily mean that you're not going through a dark night, but it is just as true, and as crucial to know, that seeking therapy, or taking medication for a biochemical affliction, doesn't necessarily mean you have subverted your spiritual process or numbed your reality sense with muffling anesthetics. It is unrealistic to believe that any honest consideration of the night in our day and age can blink away the tares-and-wheat nature of the two conditions growing side by side in the field of many souls.

In any case, if we are not prepared to consider the possibility that what we are suffering is "just" inadequate serotonin reuptake, an Oedipal knot or attachment disorder, or a simple failure to buck up properly and see the glass as half full, we can be sure that those who love us will raise the issues for us.

One of the comforters who were among Job's greatest torments was Zophar the Namathite, who advised Job to examine his soul and root out his iniquities and "put them far away": "Then surely you could lift up your face without spot; yes, you could be steadfast, and not fear.... And your life would be brighter than noonday."

It is worth noting that the humanistic solution to existential distress has not changed much in three thousand years. Zophar was recommending an attitude adjustment, essentially, a return to right thinking: Get your head on straight, man, for God's sake. He probably had some self-help books on his shelf, and all manner of ancient Hebrew techniques to accentuate the positive, eliminate the negative, and don't mess with Mr. In-Between.

Zophar is also, perhaps, the one who would tell Job now, in the general eclipse of our sense of coming to terms with Yahweh's conditions: Get professional help. A little therapy can work wonders.

It is a pretty sure thing that almost anyone could profit by the self-examination and analysis of psychotherapy, recognizing and releasing unconscious compulsions, touching old wounds and experiencing the healing of conscious suffering and forgiveness, and becoming more decent and authentic human beings in the process.

It is also true that the process of stripping away the self's unreal image of itself cannot properly take place in the absence of a viable, working ego in the first place. We have to be somebody before we can begin to be nobody. One of the major fallacies of the overeager spiritual seeker is the notion that since it is our ego that causes our suffering, we must destroy our ego. But even the attempted destruction of the ego is the ego's work, and there is nothing more obnoxious than some guy passing himself off as God's latest hollow reed.

At the same time, there are real and distinct limits to what psychotherapy can accomplish. Freud put it beautifully: the aim of psychoanalysis is to help the patient let go of the delusional suffering of his neuroses and experience the misery of actual reality. The best we can hope for under our own steam is to be modest and realistic in our ordinary sinfulness as we try our ordinary human best to be decent.

But the dark night is not a higher order of psychotherapy; it is not some final and supereffective fixing of the ego. We need not be free of neurosis or even simple wrong-headedness to experience the dark night: the contorted life paths of any number of warped saints and twisted holy people testify eloquently enough to this. The recognition of the emptiness of the self and its projects without God's sustaining grace is a different order of experience entirely. The fruit of therapy is at best a realistic sense of one's true, irreducible value among other selves and in oneself, and a realistic uncondemnatory awareness of one's limits as an ego among egos, based on compassionate self-knowledge; but the fruit of the dark night is the surrender of the realistic self's ultimately mysterious meaning to God's unfathomable direction. We embrace this surrender, in the end, not because it is the right thing to do, not to become better people, and certainly not to become "brighter than noonday," but because we have realized through prolonged and often bitter experience that is the only thing to do.

In this light, Job's reply to Zophar's therapeutic advice is notable, both for the lovely, heedless lucidity of Job's exasperation and for the deeper awareness of the nature of the process he is suffering: "What you know, I also know; I am not inferior to you.... But your platitudes are proverbs of ashes, your defenses are defenses of clay": "Who among you does not know that the hand of the Lord has done this, in whose hand is the life of every living thing, and the breath of all mankind?"

And Job concludes, in a classic formulation of the surrender necessary in the abyss of the soul's helplessness, beyond all therapeutic avail: "Though God slay me, yet will I trust him."

Job's comforters are reasonable, upright, pious men, and there is much of truth and wisdom in what they offer their suffering friend. Where they fall short is in their need to believe in the comprehensibility of Job's suffering, in the smugness of their conceit that they can explain the ways of God to him and to themselves, and in their complacent sense that human efforts can suffice to end such suffering. In seeking comfort and security in a reasonable God and a tidy creation that can be comprehended, they must defend themselves against the glaring truth of Job's condition. It is Job alone, in the depths of his utterly disproportionate misery, who sees God truly: God stripped of all that human sense can make of him.

We do no one any good by encouraging a schizophrenic, a serial killer, or someone with a brain tumor to see their affliction as a dark night of the soul. But most of us fall somewhere on the semifunctional side of the line that marks the purely medical condition or untreatable character disorder. Often, too, depression is symptomatic of a Gordian knot of social dysfunctionality, and the communal compulsion to treat the "identified patient" with drugs to "solve the problem" (and thus avoid examining the pathological elements of the social matrix itself) is strong. At various times through my own years of depression I was strongly urged to take antidepressants, but the social dynamic at those points was such that to do so would have felt like capitulation, surrender to a form of coercion. You may simply be the canary in the coal mine, the first to succumb to a bad atmosphere. I once saw a wonderful Gary Larsen cartoon in which a cow was lying on a therapy couch, with a cow therapist attentively taking notes in the background. "I don't know, Doc," the cow-patient was saying. "Sometimes I think it's not me, it's the herd."

The point is, life is complex. Doubt as to whether you are in a dark night or "just depressed" is probably a very good sign; it means you're alive and paying attention and that life has you baffled, which is the precondition for truth in my experience. It's uncomfortable, but the more we learn to live with that discomfort—to just breathe and be amid the terror of uncertainty—the more reality can sing us its subtler songs. You may well be helped through your brutal moods or your bogged-down lows by prescription drugs; you probably need therapy (I attend my weekly sessions religiously); and your childhood was almost certainly a mess; but what Viktor Frankl says in his wonderful book *The Doctor and the Soul* is likely still true for you: "The 'symptom' of conscientious anxiety in the melancholiac is not the product of melancholia as a physical illness ... [but] represents an 'accomplishment' of the human being as a spiritual person. It is understandable only as the anxiety of a human being as such: as existential anxiety."

In general, it is fruitless to treat such existential anxiety as an obstacle. It is more like the coastal fog of northern California, a natural product of prevailing conditions. The cold Humboldt current of the usual self meets the warm land mass of God—or reality, if you will—and the fog of anxiety arises. We cannot wait for the weather to change before we begin to live. The weather is beyond our control, and the climate of our lives is to be lived in, not changed. The journey to the bottom of the self is a risky one, whatever you call it, and while it may be true that ultimately the best course probably lies between the Scylla of a reductionistic psychiatry and the Charybdis of an arrogant "spirituality," all we really have is a way of traveling, however we map the sea of suffering in which we find ourselves. We are, inescapably, large-brained mammals with messy biochemistries; we are social beings riddled with the symptoms of civilization and its discontents; and we are spiritual animals subject to all the ills the soul is heir to. Our souls and selves do not develop under laboratory conditions; we mature toward our divine equilibrium in the real world, with its inevitable commingling of our neuroses, social dysfunctions, and simple life noise.

One thing is certain, whatever choices we make: we will not miss out on some crucial purgation by seeking treatment for depression or any other form of physical suffering. If we are ripe for what the dark night brings, God will find a way to bring the process to fruition no matter how hard we try to avoid it.

six

Then you pray the prayer that is the essence
of every ritual: God,
I have no hope. I am torn to shreds. You are my first and
my last and only refuge.
Don't do daily prayers like a bird pecking, moving its head
up and down. Prayer is an egg.
Hatch out the total helplessness inside.

—RUMI

"The dark night is not an abstract notion on some list of experiences every seeker is supposed to have," writes Mirabai Starr. "The dark night descends on a soul when everything else has failed. When she is no longer the best meditator in the class because her meditation produces absolutely nothing. When prayer evaporates on her tongue and she has nothing left to say to God. When she is not even tempted to return to a life of worldly pleasure

because the world has proven empty and yet taking another step through the void of the spiritual life seems futile
because she is no good at it and it seems that God has given
up on her anyway."

It is humiliating. We fast, we pray, we take up a mar-
tial art. We spice our diet with ginseng and eat only vegetables grown in Zen monastery gardens. If we have been
meditating an hour a day, we meditate two; we hang the
appropriate crystals and buy new furniture to address the
nagging issue of feng shui. We see a past-life therapist. But
none of it is any fun. The fountain that bubbled within us
has gone dry, and we're just going through the dusty mo-
tions now.

"We must not minimize the fact that this is a genuine
risk," Thomas Merton cautions: we "may not be able to
face the terrible experience of being apparently without
faith in order to really grow in faith." But "it is this test-
ing, this fire of purgation, that burns out the human and
accidental elements of faith in order to liberate the deep
spiritual power in the center of our being."

Merton adds that the dark night, with its agonies and its dangers, is, however impossible it may be to see this during the process itself, "a gift of God." Quoting Isaac of Stella, a twelfth-century Cistercian monk, he insists that it is an *inferno, sed misericordiae, non irae:* a hell of mercy, not of wrath.

He was right, too: it *was* impossible to see that during the process itself. *Misericordiae, irae,* gift of God, whatever: a hell's a hell when you're in it.

A teaching story from the Judeo-Christian wisdom tradition: It seems that one fine day in heaven, St. Peter and Moses are out for a round of golf. They come to the beautiful ninth hole on the Heaven Course number 2, a long par 3 with a lake. St. Peter hits first, a conservative two-iron that ends up hole-high on the fat side of the green. Moses says, "Nice shot, Pete," and takes a five-iron out of his own bag. St. Peter reminds him about the length of the water carry, but Moses says, "Don't worry, I once saw Arnold Palmer hit five-iron on exactly this kind of hole and stick it two feet from the pin."

So he hits his shot cleanly and it sails upward beauti-fully and lands right in the middle of the lake. Moses says, "Darn, darn, darn," or something to that effect, and walks over to the lake and strikes the waters with his driver. The lake parts, and he retrieves his ball and walks back to the ninth tee. He tees it up again, still with the five-iron, and Peter says, "Uh, Moses—" and Moses says, "No, no, I'm telling you, man, I've seen Arnold Palmer make this shot a dozen times."

So he whales away with the five-iron, and the ball sails out on a perfect arc, dead on line, and lands right in the middle of the lake. And Moses says, "Phooey, phooey, phooey," or words to that effect in Hebrew. And Peter says, "Look, Moses, if only out of compassion for the ducks, try the two-iron." But Moses just shakes his head and stalks over and parts the waters again. He retrieves his ball, stomps back to the ninth tee, and tees it up yet again, still with that darned five-iron.

By this time there's a backup behind them, two groups impatiently waiting to play through. Of course they've noticed all the superfluous parting of the waters. And one of the guys gripes to St. Peter, "Who does that guy think he is, Moses or something?" And St. Peter says, "Actually, he *is* Moses. He *thinks* he's Arnold Freakin' Palmer."

⁓

A sense of genuine helplessness dawns slowly, like a sunrise in a rainstorm. We are prodigiously resourceful animals, and it is not until our bags of tricks turn inside out that we are able to suspect, even briefly, that our muscular spiritual egos, the objects of so much self-improvement, have failed us. It's just not something we want to know about. We all think we're Arnold Freakin' Palmer, spiritually speaking, and we are determined to drive that green. We've worked too hard to consider that it's all been "for nothing."

But a full insight into the hopelessness and inescapability of our situation is the first real fruit of the purgative night. Even our most sincere attempts at self-transcendence are colored with self. It is only in the full experience of our bind, of the impossibility of self-help at this level, that we are reduced to genuine humility and prepared for grace.

"No matter how much an individual does through his own efforts," John of the Cross says, "he cannot actively purify himself enough to be disposed in the least degree for the divine union of the perfection of love." What the dark night shows us, through the intensely resisted revelation of our spiritual bankruptcy, is that we have been in the game for the payoff; we've accumulated spiritual experience on the basis of sound advice and made considered investments of time and energy as we might build a stock portfolio. We've been hoping for peace of mind during our golden years, a solid foundation of spiritual capital, security, and a 9 percent return of bliss. But now the bottom has fallen out of the market. Our spiritual checks are bouncing.

❧

My own instinct at this point was to try even harder. I felt that I had gotten this far through my own determined spiritual efforts, and those efforts were the only way I knew to move forward, which I was still sure was the point. "The suffering on the path is the ego giving up its belief in autonomy, its belief that it is the ruler," Llewellyn Vaughan-Lee notes in *Bond with the Beloved*. And the ego does not give up until it has tried everything, and tried it again, and then tried it more intensely.

For more than twenty years I had prided myself on surviving as a writer. No matter how bad things got, I would raise my meager quota of pages like the flag at Fort McHenry in "The Star-Spangled Banner": by the rocket's red glare, I would offer my tattered art to the world. It was the symbol of my endurance, if nothing else; and my sense of vocation, of doing the work that God had given me, was my rock. Secretly, I never really let go of the notion that all this faithfulness would lead to a happy ending in the finest literary tradition: that I would end up on the best-seller lists, that the world would eventually kiss the frog of my obscure little books and find a prince.

Now, in the brutal clarity of the night, I began for the first time to consider that God had called me not to a path of vindication and the trumpets of success but to failure, and to silence. Because silence was the deepest truth of my existence now. After years of listening to a thread of inner music, I couldn't hear a thing. The choruses of doubt and despair were still going strong, but I had always been able to find my way past that blare into the country of quiet song that is a writer's sustaining home. Now, even when I managed through surrender, cunning, or pure dumb luck to slip beyond the din of negativity, there was only silence, a silence so complete, in an inward stillness so vast and seemingly final, that there was no appeal.

"Empty yourself of *everything*," Meister Eckhart says. "That is to say, empty yourself of your ego and empty yourself of all things and of all that you are in yourself and consider yourself as what you are in God. God is a being beyond being and a nothingness beyond being. Therefore, be still, and do not flinch from this emptiness."

I inevitably *would* flinch, of course; I would panic and try new tricks, anything to get out of that terrifying hush; but always when the fresh spasm of resistance had used itself up, the silence was there. Like cliffs of stone, like the desert and the sky. It was increasingly clear that I wasn't going to be able to wiggle out of this one. Eventually, from sheer exhaustion, I began to try to learn to live with it.

———

I had remarried in 1993, to a marvelous and gifted woman. The marriage was a sort of longshot miracle of belated normality for both of us: We had met in a group marriage commune in the Haight, sharing the ordeals and adventures of that experience, and monogamy was a radical experiment. But it seemed to suit us both. We spent our early years together in San Francisco, but my mother's illness throughout 1997 exerted an extraordinary gravitational force, drawing us back to the east coast, where we both had our roots. Following Mom's death that Christmastime, Claire and I moved to tidewater Virginia, trading in the scrap of grass and garden behind our in-law apartment in San Francisco for an old farmhouse and two acres of weeds amid soybean fields and swamps.

I had brought my psychic work-in-progress with me, of course. It's not the sort of thing you can leave at your previous apartment, along with the almost empty bottles of Windex, nail holes in the wall, and half a can of paint under the sink, figuring that the cleaning deposit will cover it. If anything, the rural isolation and the loss of my social matrix intensified my condition. I sat at my writing desk with a view of the Back Bay every morning for my ritual four hours and didn't produce a thing; reduced to inarticulate prayers for mercy and messy wrestling with the demons of despair, I watched literal dust settle on my work in progress, slow motes drifting onto the pages out of shafts of morning sun. In the afternoon I pushed a lawnmower around and around our infinite lawn in the soggy tidewater heat, and in the evening I drank a beer or two, watched the nightly news like everyone else in America, and tried to be decent to my loving and long-suffering wife.

I had learned at last to not project my darkness onto those around me; I knew perfectly well that I had a good marriage with a wonderful woman, a beautiful home, and the only job I had ever wanted. I had a life that most of the people on the planet would trade for in a second, but all that it meant in practice was that there was nowhere left to run. I'd lost my sense that any of it meant anything, and I hadn't written a word for almost a year. It seemed to me that in just about every way that mattered I had simply disappeared.

———

If you had asked me, at just about any point along my tortuous spiritual path, I would have said of such self-disappearance, "Bring it on." Transcending the ego, escaping from the suffering self, had always seemed like the Holy Grail, the pearl of great price, the prize at the end of the spiritual bingo game. "Except a kernel of wheat fall into the ground and die, it abideth alone," Jesus tell us in the Gospel of John. "But if it die, it bringeth forth much fruit." I had longed for that spiritual death.

But be careful what you ask for—there is a reason that almost every spiritual tradition tells some version of the fable of the wish-fulfilling tree that grants the naive seeker all his desires, to his eventual deep chagrin. The country of selflessness, of nothingness, of letting go of the ego project, is dangerous terrain. It is not a place we could imagine when we began our spiritual journey.

"Beauty is a simple passion," Anne Sexton warns us in her poetry, "but, oh my friends, in the end, / You will dance the fire in iron shoes." The scriptures and the writings of the mystics are full of sobering admonitions about the ultimate price of the spiritual path, trying to prepare us for what T. S. Eliot calls "a condition of complete simplicity / (Costing not less than everything)." But the truth is there is no way to be prepared for the cross; we have no referents in our usual lives for such finality of surrender. Because Meister Eckhart liked to talk about the nothingness of the divine and prayed to God to relieve him of "God," the Church of his day was prepared to burn him at the stake as a heretic and an atheist. Fortunately he died of natural causes before they could, and so he is now a pillar of mystical theology. Marguerite Porete, who was not so fortunate, or perhaps was simply less discreet—or maybe just too female—died in the flames at the Church's hands at about the same time for stretching the limits of theistic language by noting that "the annihilated Soul is so transparent in understanding that she sees herself to be nothing in God and God nothing in her."

Moreover, the self has myriad cunning disguises, and more often than not a willed "selflessness" can sneak in rather than the spontaneous exhaustion of self that leaves room for God's movement. We will always have to have a working ego, in any case, as we will always have to wear clothes despite our naturally naked condition, and for the same reason: to move around in the social world as a participant. The closest I ever got to pure "selflessness" was right before I ended up in four-point restraints on Ward 7-B at San Francisco General; coincidentally or not, I also was inclined to take off my clothes at the drop of a hat (so to speak) during that time.

～

"The problem with talking about enlightenment is that our talk tends to create a picture of what it is," says Joko Beck in *Everyday Zen*. "Yet enlightenment is not a picture but the shattering of all our pictures. And a shattered life isn't what we were hoping for."

Selflessness—our essential nothingness—is the deepest truth of our being; God works in us where we cease to exist. But the painful truth is that, much as we have believed we will welcome that shattering of ego and God's free working in us—much, indeed, as we have believed that is precisely what we are trying to accomplish with all our spiritual heroics—we will fight that ego death when it comes with everything we have. To the ego, the silence of God is nothing, empty; it is not what we want, not what we thought, and there's nothing we can do.

A friend of mine once asked me if I knew what INRI, the letters tacked above Jesus's head on the cross, meant. Being the spiritual wonk that I am, I said smugly, "*Iesus Nazarenus Rex Iudaeorum.*" And she said, "No. It means, 'I'm Nailed Right In.'"

Yet it is here, nailed right in to this nowhere, where we are helpless and can do nothing, that everything arises, mysteriously. There is nowhere else to go and nothing else to do but make our peace with it. Much as it pains us to realize it, our ultimate unselfing is not for us to accomplish.

The crucifixion can come gently or horrifically, but in any case we will pray in the end, as Jesus did, for God to take the cup away, before we surrender and ask that God's will, not ours, be done.

"So the abyss . . . ," Theodore Roethke says, in his marvelous poem of that name:

> A flash into the burning heart of the abominable;
> Yet if we wait, unafraid, beyond the fearful instant,
> The burning lake turns into a forest pool,
> The fire subsides into rings of water,
> A sunlit silence.

The blessing in this storm is that, sink or swim, we're in God's hands. You will be graced with the disaster your soul requires to find its way home. There is really nothing for you to accomplish except the ongoing work of trust, patience (a word rooted etymologically in passion, in suffering), and surrender to what is. And what is, is ultimately merciful. I don't say this lightly; God knows, I hate that Pollyanna shit as much as the next person.

seven

When we have reached this total deprivation,
what shall we do? Abide in simplicity and peace,
as Job on his ash-heap, repeating "Blessed are the poor
in spirit; those who have nothing have all,
since they have God."

—JEAN-PAUL DE CAUSSADE

There is an old joke about a farmer who decided to save money by teaching his horse to go without food. He cut down on the poor beast's ration of oats day by day; the horse, being a horse, plodded on stolidly, if somewhat lethargically, and the plan seemed to be working pretty well. The farmer was soon saving twenty dollars a week. Unfortunately, just about the time he had gotten the horse trained to go without food entirely, the damn thing died.

I felt that God was performing a similar experiment with me. I missed my oats of joy, inspiration, and meaning;

of art, and the making of art; of love itself: of everything that makes life worth living. I really wasn't good for anything anymore except surrender. For perhaps five minutes a day as the months after my mother's death turned into years, my fevered brain would cool into acceptance, and I would grow calm and peaceful, reconciled to my nothingness, a contented citizen in the country of silence. It didn't seem like much to base a career on.

"Everything depends on this: a fathomless sinking in a fathomless nothingness," Johannes Tauler, a fourteenth-century mystic, offers helpfully. His contemporary, John Ruusbroec, is similarly specific: "We must place our entire life on the foundation of a groundless abyss."

A fathomless nothingness and a groundless abyss. If you have reached the point where this makes any sense at all to you, God help you. Because you are finally prepared to understand that no one and nothing else can. We have, in the deepest sense, arrived. And we are nowhere.

My "writing routine" had long since grown paradoxical, in that it produced no writing whatsoever beyond smudges in my journal and, given the wild swings between terror, despair, and acceptance, was anything but routine. But I kept coming to the desk every morning anyway, and I am convinced, in retrospect, that this is a key element in the dark night reaching critical mass: having something, anything, that you will continue to do just for the doing of it, long after every possible reason to do it has evaporated, a leap of faith you are willing to take even after it has become clear that it really does just go straight off that cliff and you're not a hero or a saint or anything even remotely edifying, you're a freakin' idiot and they're going to spell your name wrong on your gravestone.

I had started out as a classic mystical-mojo writer, an inspiration junky, a numinosity hound, and had more or less systematically associated God with the holy hush that is the prelude to actual sentences bubbling out. It was the fuel I ran on. I had learned pretty much every route there was into a certain contemplative Stillness and knew every inner trick to invoke it; I had made a cult of one out of ecstatic Silence, and it had taken me a remarkably long way, but all I could think of now when I considered that journey was a cartoon I had seen once, of a cat crammed hopelessly into a jar, with a caption that read, "Cat, having worked very hard to get somewhere, wondering where exactly it is that she has gotten."

There was no question of backing out. I still felt God had led me into this jar. I just figured he was perverse or that I was the only soul in the history of the human race to be beyond salvation. In any case, an entire lifetime of working states that had carried a positive affective charge had been drained of all their juice and turned into binding pain. What I had to slowly learn to do now was to let go of all my routes and stop doing all my tricks, to simply be in the stillness and the silence without the guiding glow and the certainty of the Sacred. I was being weaned, essentially, from numinosity. It felt like dying, but not a glamorous mystical dying into an obvious and inwardly palpable heaven: just dying, into a cold grave.

It sounds bizarre, but I think the key point in the dark night is basically everything but this death being hell. I was still, silent, perfectly accepting at last, inwardly, only because it hurt so much to move. It didn't feel good or holy or anything much, but it didn't hurt. It was not peace, in any positive sense, at least not for a very long time, but it was quiet and painless, and for me at that point, after years of every spiritual effort causing only pain, frustration, dryness, and inner noise, that quiet—not Quiet, just quiet—would do just fine.

It is unnerving to glimpse the life beyond the self. Nothing has changed. The world is still an infinite desert to us. We are still useless, hopeless, and helpless. According to all our ego's criteria, we should be six feet under, with our loved ones standing sadly around the grave reciting the Twenty-third Psalm and hoping that our soul finds the comfort in the hereafter that it never found on earth. But here we are, still breathing in the darkness, immersed in a secret peace. The worst has happened, and it turns out to be a surprisingly lovely, quiet thing.

And so we abide in that abyss, not even knowing why at this point, defeated, surrendered, and undone. We pray through the night, though prayer seems meaningless; we listen for the spirit's song through that silence at 3 a.m., when all words fail; we love when love seems most defeated and pointless. By now we are convinced that these things will almost certainly accomplish nothing at all. But we do them anyway. We pray, for no reason besides the praying, and we listen for the sacred music, for the sake of the holy listening only, and we love, simply for the loving itself.

"I have a feeling that my boat / has struck, down here in the depths, / against a great thing," Juan Ramón Jiménez writes, in a poem beautifully translated by Robert Bly:

> And nothing
> happens! Nothing ... Silence ... Waves ...
> —Nothing happens? Or has everything happened
> and we are standing now, quietly, in the new life?

There *is* a sense of standing quietly now in a new life. You try to tell your friends and family, who've been so worried about you. But in the telling it sounds dishearteningly morbid. The embrace of a fathomless nothingness is not exactly the American dream. In fact, it sounds suspiciously like diagnostic criterion number two for a Major Depressive Episode in the APA's *Manual for Mental Disorders.* There's still not a damn thing you can see worth doing in the whole wide world. It's just that you've made your peace with that.

So you go back to your secret quiet, deep inside your cocoon of misery. And you think, in that lovely hush, So this is what it's like to be dead. It's really not so bad.

"I rock between dark and dark, / My soul nearly my own, / My dead selves singing," Roethke writes in "The Abyss":

> And I embrace this calm—
> Such quiet beneath the small leaves!—
> Near the stem, whiter at root,
> A luminous stillness.

Last year at my church, St. Aidan's Episcopal in Virginia Beach, we decided to take a chance with our children's

Lenten program and do a kid-friendly Stations of the Cross. There was initially some concern that incomprehensible condemnation, savage scourging, and relentless suffering unto death might not be appropriate material for pre-K-through-second-grade kids, but in the end the children's walk with Jesus, including the holy limbo at station 4.5 and the sacred hopscotch after the second fall, went wonderfully. We got everyone corralled and costumed, set things up with Matthew 16:24, and off we went. A fourth-grade Pilate condemned the younger kids to death, the adult soldiers in period garb crowned them with pipe-cleaner thorns, and they took up their crosses and followed Jesus to Golgotha, two hallways over, collecting their Stations of the Cross Trading Cards along the way.

For the last stages, the kids passed one by one through a black veil and were bombarded with black confetti and stripped of their robes by seventh-grade soldiers. They suffered, died, and were carried into an amazingly constructed tomb, complete with a tomb keeper to orient them, where they received their final trading cards and a glitter-filled cocoon that opened to reveal candy, a butterfly, and a fortune-cookie-like slip that said, "I have been crucified with Christ, but still I live; though it is no longer I, but it is Christ who lives in me" (Galatians 2:19–20).

Later, while the vacuum cleaner was choking on the glitter and confetti, one of the little girls, a second-grader named Dana, was telling her mother and me how terrible it had been in the tomb, hot and crowded, sixteen squirming kids and a couple of adults all crammed into a dark, tiny space. Her mother said, "Yeah, just think of poor Jesus. He had to be all alone in *his* tomb." And Dana said, "Lucky Jesus!"

⸺

"Where shall wisdom be found?" Job asks. "And where is the place of understanding? Man knoweth not the price thereof; neither is it found in the land of the living."

Lucky Jesus, alone in his tomb, is perhaps the ultimate spiritual paradox. The price of wisdom is the grave, beyond everything we know of the land of the living, but the grave is not the end. The promise of this is perfectly explicit, everywhere in wisdom literature and scripture, but it is only in a tomb of one's own that we are finally prepared to take that promise literally: "Whosoever will save his life shall lose it; and whosoever will lose his life for my sake shall find it."

This is not some extreme and esoteric spiritual truth available only to a few elite fanatics and saints. Anyone who has tasted real grief, real despair, real depression, knows what it means to be as good as dead. One way or another, life will bring us to this point of feeling we have nothing left to lose, in spite our best efforts to avoid it. But the miracle of this thing we call death is that it is only in our seemingly final defeat, only through suffering the annihilation of everything we know and think ourselves to be, that we find ourselves capable at last of knowing God's real mercy.

Elijah, in a tomblike cave on a lonely mountain, waiting for God to answer his desperate prayer, had a great wind pass over him, but the Lord was not in the wind; and then an earthquake came, but not God; and finally a tremendous fire. "But the Lord was not in the fire; and after the fire, a still, small voice" (1 Kings 19:12).

It is in the silence of the tomb that we can hear the still, small voice of God with perfect clarity at last. Nothing is needed here, and there is nothing to do; and no one to need it and no one to do it. There is only the endless fall into the unfathomable mystery of God's presence, here and now and always.

Nice work, if you can get it. For a lazy man like me, it seemed almost like cheating.

eight

Inside this new love, die.
Your way begins on the other side.
... Die,
and be quiet. Quietness is the surest sign
that you've died.
Your old life was a frantic running
from silence.
The speechless full moon
comes out now.
—RUMI

The Stations of the Cross traditionally end in the pregnant stillness of the tomb at the fourteenth station. The Resurrection is implied, and the life of the resurrected soul is left to our imagination. The stone rolls away from the entrance, the dawn light seeps in, we take a tentative step toward the world on untested feet, and—what? God knows. The fruits of silence and a journey as deep as the dark night don't ripen for our convenience; they have their own timetable. Deep-sea divers have to come up slowly and wait through long periods of decompression so that the concentrated nitrogen in their blood can diffuse. If they try to reenter normal atmospheric conditions prematurely, nitrogen bubbles form in their bloodstream and give them "the bends."

I've come to think of this interregnum period, this baffling, passive, peaceful pause between the failure of the ego's furious projects and the first singing of compassion's unfathomable grace, as something analogous at the soul level. We move gently, and even imperceptibly, back toward the surface world after a prolonged immersion in the depths while the silence in which we have dissolved reformulates our life into something that can bear the weight of normal gravity.

It was at about this time, I remember, that I was standing outside in the dark one early morning, taking a break from my predawn "writing" routine, looking up at the three-quarter-full moon being caressed by the darkened edges of some slow-sailing clouds, and a moth flew right into my glasses. He'd taken the reflection in the lenses for a living light—very Zen. He flew off at once, a little freaked out. And I just thought, Yeah, you and me too, buddy.

It was actually disorienting to me by now to not be in acute misery. I had always thought that when such peace came, it would be accompanied by an obvious and even spectacular Direction; like the Blues Brothers, we all want to be on a mission from God. But this peace seemed to require nothing of me.

"This plateau is actually our time of becoming rooted in silence," Bernadette Roberts says, "rooted until this silence becomes the deepest, most stable habit of soul, the deepest aspect of our existence." There's nothing else to do: "We have been too burnt to move, learned too well the lesson: of ourselves we can do nothing. The only choice is to remain patient, silent, and to be resigned to this state as long as God wills."

It was still possible to be wretched—all I had to do to suffer, indeed, was to picture myself doing anything at all. The merest hint of a projected course of action or grasping for meaning sufficed to throw me right back into the heart of the fire; and my mind regularly threw up its usual quotient of schemes, plans, and scenarios. My emotions continued to surge and ebb as well, and in particular at this time I was often overwhelmed by an almost unbearable sense of poignancy. But the difference now was that peace was possible; it was there for the having, and it took nothing to be peaceful but the practice of the simplest—albeit clueless—stillness. I was learning to live in the country of silence. It seemed to me for quite a while that I would never do anything else, and that actually seemed okay. Life goes on, but sometimes it goes on without us for a time.

—◆—

In January of the brand-new millennium, two years after my mother's death, an old friend called from San Francisco to wish me happy new year. A painter whose work I loved, she and I had been classmates in the school of depression for years, swapping tales of our darker hours with rueful camaraderie.

Now, it appeared, April had graduated. Her voice was bright, strong, and full of laughter. She was pulling together a major show, surviving the wreck of a relationship with wisdom and humor, and painting beautifully. She had joined a gym and she was buff. She was having breakthroughs in therapy. And, oh, yeah, by the way: she had finally taken the plunge and started taking an antidepressant called Something-Something.

"It's changed my life," she told me. "I wish I'd started taking it twenty years ago."

It wasn't, of course, the first time I'd considered the notion of chemical assistance. You aren't as fucked up as I had been for as long as I was without a lot of people telling you you should be on drugs. I'd been shot full of Haldol to break a mania, swaddled in sedatives to blunt the breakage, and spoon-fed lithium to reconstruct a durable decorum. I'd had relationships in which the women made going on antidepressants a condition of staying in the relationship, and I had left those relationships. I'd been handed any number of Xeroxed articles on Prozac, Wellbutrin, and the new generation of serotonin reuptake inhibitors. I'd even gone so far as to try St. John's wort and had eaten endless vitamins. But this was the first time I had heard the chemical gospel preached by an artist whose creative process was an inspiration to me and who could assure me that the drugs hadn't messed her up.

The next day I told my wife that I was thinking of seeing a psychiatrist and asking about antidepressants. She nodded supportively, ducked her head, and began to quietly sob from gratitude and relief. She'd been praying for me to ask for professional help for a year and a half. It's hell living with a depressed person.

A week later I was in the office of a chipper little woman with a prescription pad who briefed me on the laundry list of potential side effects and recommended Effexor—a phenethylamine bicyclic derivative, the woman explained helpfully, as opposed to the monoamine oxidase inhibitors. I nodded humbly and got my prescription filled at the Kmart pharmacy on the way home.

A good proportion of the side effects duly occurred, but about a week after I started on the drug I was driving home one afternoon with a bag of groceries and a pack of cigarettes and I noticed how beautiful the winter trees were in the crystalline February light. That got my attention all right. It seemed like forever since I had noticed any trees.

Would my "dark night" have ended without drugs? Not when it did, certainly. This bothered me quite a bit, until a friend of mine told me a joke. It seems that there was this guy who lived beside a river. One day a hard rain fell in the mountains, and the water upstream began to rise. Flood warnings were broadcast on television and radio, but the guy ignored them, saying, "God will take care of me." As the water began to rise in his yard, a man on a bicycle peddled by and shouted that he had better pack up and leave, that the flood was coming. But the guy said, "No, it's okay, God will take care of me."

Soon the water had reached his porch; it poured into his living room and started coming up the stairs. The guy climbed out onto his roof, and another man in a boat paddled by and told him to hop in. "No, thanks, God will take care of me," the guy told him, and the man in the boat shook his head and paddled on.

Finally even the rooftop was awash. The guy climbed into a nearby tree, praying pretty hard by now, clinging to the branches as they swayed in the torrent. A helicopter drew near and a rope was lowered, but the guy hollered over the rotor noise, "It's okay! God will take care of me!" And so, of course, he drowned.

When he got to heaven, he went straight to God and asked him what the hell had happened, why he hadn't been saved by his faith.

"I don't know," God told him. "I'm as baffled as you. I sent you those reports on the radio and TV, I sent the guy on the bicycle and the guy in the boat, and finally I sent a helicopter. What more did you want from me?"

I think my friend's New Year's phone call was a saving gift from God. I think God sent the indomitable little woman with the prescription pad and that by God's grace I was desperate enough by then to grab the lifeline. I think the Kmart pharmacy is an outpost of heaven. The dark night is not about suffering for suffering's sake; it is about a certain work of soul being accomplished. When the work is done, it is time to move on.

—◦—

I knew perfectly well that I had accomplished nothing. Stanislav Grof tells of a middle-aged woman who had gone through what he calls the "ego-death experience," who said, "Afterward, someone congratulated me on my courage at putting the pieces of myself back together. But there were no pieces left, not even a shred. Everything I thought I was had been demolished." This was true. My old self had melted away like cotton candy in the rain, but I had no sense at all of having actively fashioned a new one. And yet somehow the bills were getting paid and the grass was getting cut.

Three months after I started on Effexor, the novel that had been stalled for a year and a half was finished. I was socializing with my family and friends again and making new friends. I was teaching Sunday school to first-graders and could tell them without rolling my eyes that God was a good and merciful God. I felt that my life had been given back to me in an immeasurably heightened way. Even taking flowers to my mother's grave, I was filled with a sense of gratitude and joy. I still missed her, of course—missed her laughter and her stories and the sheer vigor of her spirit; I even missed her terrible driving. But the grief was warm and sweetened now, like honeyed tea, a liquid, gentle heat within. I wished she could have stuck around to see her son grow up.

nine

No one is so advanced in prayer
that they do not often have to return to the beginning.
—ST. TERESA OF AVILA

Being, not doing, is my first joy.
—THEODORE ROETHKE, "THE ABYSS"

So, it's Lent, Ash Wednesday, and this parish priest gets
hit with a wave of humility, in the spirit of the season.
He falls to his knees before the altar and begins beating
his breast and praying fervently, "Oh, Lord, I'm nothing,
I'm *nothing*." And this goes on for some time, until his
assistant rector comes in. The assistant sees his boss beating his breast, and he is inspired to fall to his own knees
beside him, and he too begins to pray, "I'm nothing, O
God, I'm nothing." And they're both nothing, and this
goes on, and after a while the janitor comes in and he sees

these guys going at it and he is inspired too, and he too falls to his knees and begins to pray from the depths of his heart, "I'm nothing, O God, I'm nothing." And the assistant priest nudges the rector and says, "Look who thinks *he's* nothing."

"Enlightenment is not what it was ever imagined to be by the ego," Mariana Caplan writes. In her book *Halfway Up the Mountain: The Error of Premature Claims to Enlightenment,* she explores with masterful thoroughness the myriad ways in which the project of transcendence of the self can be co-opted to the ends of the ego. The "upper" reaches of the path are, if anything, even more dangerous than the more obvious and standard pitfalls of greedy beginners; having acquired a store of increasingly sophisticated "spiritual" experience, we grow capable of ever subtler self-delusion. Without a corrective, even the highest of satoris and samadhis can be made grist for the ego's mill. Reduced fleetingly to something like the divine zero, humbled to the brink of annihilation, we recover and start showing off our nothingness. We broadcast our silence everywhere: Look how silent I am! We manifest a rose and promptly open a flower stand.

The dark night of the spirit, as understood by John of the Cross, is specifically purgative of this subtler "spiritual" selfishness, which is ineradicable through the self's own efforts. That John of the Cross is a Doctor of the Church is a joke, in a way, because no one really accepts his diagnosis. He's a sixteenth-century maniac with a thirteenth-century vocabulary; his teachings are daunting, demanding, uncompromising, and relentless, and you have to be extraordinarily miserable before you can really begin to appreciate him. Not exactly the stuff of best sellers in an age of spiritual quick fixes. And the ones who do open up to the truth of what John is saying do so only kicking and screaming all the way.

John strikes a deathblow to the notion that the deepest spirituality is something we can *do,* something within the working realm of our will's control and effectiveness. The dark night is about realizing the absolute poverty of our spiritual efforts, the inevitable element of self in even the best of our goodness and striving for the light; it is about being broken by God, stripped naked of all accomplishment and all that we have taken for "meaning." It is about trusting God, not because it is the right thing or the good thing or the thing that will advance us spiritually, but because it is the only thing we can do. And to reach that point, all the right things we do and all the good things we do and all the spiritual advances we have believed ourselves to be making must be shown to us for the empty things they are.

The truth is, we *are* nothing. That is not abject humility, it's not a failure of self-esteem, it's not masochism or even a triumph of willful Christian self-mortification in the service of getting a better deal in heaven. It's just realism. But getting real is harder than we've been led to believe. The real gift, the real grace, is surrender, and surrender almost always feels like a defeat and a failure.

"The true beauty of the awakening energy is that it humiliates us," Richard Moss writes in *Words That Shine Both Ways*. "You don't become larger and grander on your own terms; you awaken and get burned. You get humbled. You get scared to death. You tremble in your bed at night."

⸺ ⸺

There is an old Buddhist story of three seekers after enlightenment, each of whom is given a magic feather that, if dropped, will allow them to remain in whatever place they are. They set off across the Ganges plain for the Himalayas in search of nirvana, intending like all beginning seekers to drop their feathers there and abide in eternal bliss. After a certain amount of hard journeying, at the farthest edge of the flatlands they come upon a kingdom where the stones themselves are silver, where every pleasure of life can be bought just for the picking up of a rock from the side of the road and suffering has been banished, and the first seeker promptly drops his feather and lives there happily ever after.

The other two, being made of sterner stuff, or perhaps simply greedier, continue up into the foothills of the Himalayas, and there, after some weeks of difficult travel, they come into a lovely green valley and find there a village where even the clods of earth are made of gold and the people abide in constant ecstasy. The second seeker drops his feather here and is instantly and completely immersed in unending bliss.

The third seeker, however, cannily noting the progression, realizes that he can do even better, and he forges on into the mountains. Clutching his feather, he passes through the high forests, braving all manner of ordeals and forgoing all manner of idyllic opportunities. He comes upon heaven after heaven of perpetual ecstasies, celestial transports, and eternal raptures, each more ambrosial and enchanting than the last. But he is determined to drop his feather only at the place of ultimate bliss.

Moving beyond the tree line, he plods upward, passing into the deep snows, through barren glacial passes and rocky slopes, until he finds himself, after months of the most intense journeying, among the icy, savage cliffs of the highest altitudes. And here, in the midst of a blinding blizzard, at the darkest hour of the coldest night he has ever known, he spies an uneasily lighted cave ahead and heads for it, seeking at least a moment's rest and a bit of respite from the bitter cold.

When the seeker enters the cave, breathing a sigh of relief simply to be out of the biting wind, he finds a lone man sitting by an inadequate fire. The man is ancient and withered and obviously spent, and on his head, like a crown of thorns, is the spinning weight of all the suffering in the world.

The seeker is so appalled by the sight that the feather he has clutched through every opportunity at earthly and unearthly paradise slips from his benumbed and frozen hand. And at that instant the spinning wheel lifts from the man's head and settles on the seeker's own, and he cries out in astonishment at the agonizing weight of all the suffering in the world.

The old man gets up and wipes the blood from his disburdened brow and bows to the seeker.

"I am grateful to you beyond words," he says.

"Wha—wha—what's going on here?" the seeker exclaims.

"A long, long time ago, like yourself, having passed through every temptation to settle for lesser truths, I came here with a feather of my own," the man tells him. "And like you, at the furthest reach of my own search for Realization, I found a man here bearing the unbearable weight of the world's suffering, and the burden passed from him to me. He told me then that I would have to remain here until another seeker came along."

Through the blood now streaming down into his own eyes, the seeker sees that the floor of the cave is littered with feathers, some of them from birds long since extinct.

"H—H—How long?" he finally manages to ask.

"What yuga is it now?" the old man replies cheerfully, and off he goes, leaving the seeker, who has arrived at last at the pinnacle of his seeking, there in the cave with the weight of the suffering world spinning relentlessly upon his head.

———

"I had a direct experience of merging with everything, of being at one with everything," Richard Moss writes. "And you want to know something? So what! It changed me physically. It changed me psychically. There was kundalini and there was this and there was that. But it didn't prepare me for loving. It didn't prepare me for divorce. It didn't prepare me for kids. It didn't prepare me for housework. The real wonderment of life is being human."

The world itself was gathered into the Word, and God was made flesh. The Word walked among us; and not I but Christ in me must walk in this world still and always. The mystery of reality in the world is terrible; we know, with Paul, that "the whole of creation groaneth and travaileth in pain until now." The ripenings that come of suffering are priceless, but the suffering still feels bad. That's why it is called suffering. Incarnation hurts, say what you will about God and love. In his later poetry John of the Cross longed frankly for the veil to be torn away completely, but he knew it wasn't going to happen while he was alive. Even Jesus prayed to have the cup of suffering taken away, but what he showed us is that the only way to do it for real is three days in the grave. No one wants to hear that suffering stops only when the breath does.

Thus the Buddha returned to the world and taught the Four Noble Truths and the Eightfold Way for forty years. So the final picture in the Zen ox-herding cycle is not of the enlightened sage established in his solitary Realization, nor even the empty circle of ultimate emptiness, but of the simple man, no longer a seeker, returning to the city with bliss-bestowing hands.

"In the Buddhist teaching the symbol for compassion is one moon shining in the sky while its image is reflected in one hundred bowls of water," Chögyam Trungpa notes. "The moon does not demand, 'If you open to me I will do you a favor and shine on you.' The moon just shines."

~

Someone—I believe it was Isaiah—once said, "Death is easy; it's comedy that's tough." The exercise of spirituality in our daily lives is seldom as spectacular as the pure form of soul struggle we find in the dark night, and our humble crises seldom have the satisfying finality of crucifixion. Our mundane crosses are much more like Sisyphus's stone, something we heave up the bloody hill through the deep mud of the petty details of our daily life, only to see it roll back down again for the labor to begin again the next day.

Bernadette Roberts tells of meeting an old woman, some time after her own dark night had run its course. During the conversation, Roberts gradually realized that the old woman, who had never undergone any formal religious training, was fully as present and immersed in God as she was herself. Roberts was struck by this: life itself had taught this woman the completeness of surrender and given her the wholeness of union—Eliot's "condition of complete simplicity / (costing not less than everything)"—bit by gradual bit, in the natural unfolding of her life.

The dark night is not something "reserved for some spiritual elite whose personalities are so strong and intact they can afford to blithely cast them into the flames of union," as Mirabai Starr points out. "Someone who is broken . . . , who has struggled all his or her life with some intense deficiency, may have a uniquely powerful relationship with God." We need not run off to a monastery or have a particular spiritual practice or even think of ourselves as "spiritual" people at all for life to bring us to the necessity for absolute surrender.

It is in that surrender, in the embrace of our own perceived futility, paradoxically, that real freedom comes. But real freedom is terrifying, and real faith is a dance, always, on the knife's edge, in unknowing. By grace, we may come to welcome the terrors of that unknowing because they are so much better than the horrors and constant anxiety of the self's small world of delusory accomplishment; by grace, we may finally prefer to be in God's darkness rather than the self's flashlight-beam-sized world with all its exclusions and blindness. And then, by grace, the whole world lights up with God and we rejoice. But the path to that gratitude and rejoicing passes through some very rough country.

❦

Denis Turner concludes his brilliant analysis of the relationship between the dark night and depression with the unencouraging assertion that while you're in one, the two are basically indistinguishable. It is only by their fruits—by their outcomes—that you can tell them apart. Depression, in retrospect, is "the revolt of the self in despair at its disintegration," while the dark night is "the dawning of a realization that in this loss of selfhood, nothing is lost; it is the awakening of the capacity to live without the need for it. When the passive nights pass, all is transformed. When depression passes, all is restored, normality is resumed, the emotional life is rehabilitated and so, for all the sufferings of the depressed, which are otherwise indistinguishable from the passive nights, nothing is gained."

The central paradox of the spiritual path is that in striving to transcend the self, we actually build it up; our holy solutions invariably calcify into grotesque casts of ego. The dark night is God's solution to our solutions, dissolving our best-laid constructions anew into the mystery of grace. It happens in spite of our best efforts to resist it. But thank God it happens.

We can treat the life-disrupting realities of depression, darkness, terror, and despair when they come (and they will) as speed bumps on the road to the usual and devote our efforts to getting back up to speed as soon as possible; or we can take the car wreck of the dark night as a grace, as what Joan Halifax calls "a sacred catastrophe" and a "holy failure." Led by suffering into the mapless country of faith, silence, and darkness, perhaps we will even glimpse the truth of what the sages and saints have been saying for ages when they talk about the necessary death of the ego and the mystery of divine life. Certainly I see my own depression, triggered by my mother's death and exacerbated by neurotic conflicts, character disorders, a chaotic temperament, and even at times borderline psychosis, as a gift of God—a hell of mercy, as the old monk said, and not of wrath.

"Oh, then, spiritual soul," John of the Cross says,

> *when you see your appetites darkened, your inclinations dry and constrained, your faculties incapacitated for any interior exercise, do not be afflicted: Think of this as a grace, since God is freeing you from yourself and your own*

activity. However well your actions may have succeeded, you did not work so perfectly and securely as you do now that God takes you by the hand and guides you in darkness, as though you were blind, along a way and to a place you know not. You would never have succeeded in reaching this place alone, no matter how good your eyes and your feet.

acknowledgments

I am grateful to Renée Sedliar, a true friend and an editor with a poet's ear, for paring away my superfluities, grounding my head trips, and drawing the best parts of this book out like blood from a wavering vein. Thanks too to Gideon Weil, my gifted editor at HarperOne, for all manner of support, sanity, and insight, and for the blessing of his friendship. My gratitude and appreciation for the wonderful HarperOne team: special thanks to Mark Tauber, Michael Maudlin, Claudia Boutote, Sam Berry, Cindy DiTiberio, and the rest of a truly rare and marvelous team of talented, funny, and literate people. Thanks to Carolyn Allison-Holland, again, for her superb shepherding skills and general siddhayogininess, and to Priscilla Stuckey for her humor and acuity, and for almost always being right.

Thanks to Claire Poole, who shared so much of this journey, and infused every adventure with light, joy, and the occasional road brew. Thank you, April Berger. God bless you, Sarah Moore. And to Marilou Kollar, my ongoing and unending thanks. I will in fact pay that whole bill, ten dollars at a time.

Thanks to Linda Chester, of the Linda Chester Literary Agency, for nearly two decades of warm and generous support. And to my agent, Laurie Fox, my beloved comrade on the road, through everything, all my gratitude and love.